W9-APG-527

a

MAD
GUIDE TO
PARENTS,
TEACHERS, AND
OTHER ENEMIES

Written by STAN HART
Illustrated by JACK DAVIS

Edited by NICK MEGLIN

WARNER BOOKS

A Warner Communications Company

WARNER BOOKS EDITION

Copyright © 1985 by Stan Hart, Jack Davis, and E.C. Publications, Inc.
All rights reserved.
No part of this book may be reproduced without permission.
For information address:
E.C. Publications, Inc.,
485 Madison Avenue,
New York, N.Y. 10022

Title "MAD" used with permission of its owner,
E.C. Publications, Inc.

This Warner Books Edition is published by
arrangement with E.C. Publications, Inc.

Warner Books, Inc.
75 Rockefeller Plaza
New York, N.Y. 10019

W A Warner Communications Company

Printed in the United States of America

First Printing: August, 1985

10 9 8 7 6 5 4 3 2 1

CONTENTS

INTRODUCTION

Don't look now, but there are enemies all around you. Hey!! We told you not to look now—they'll see you and then you'll really be in bad shape! So listen when we talk, huh? Okay! Now, there is a way to combat these enemies and the way to do that is by being informed! Remember, knowledge is power—or powder—or maybe it's pewter—whatever ... Anyway, to understand the behavior of these everyday menaces is the first step. If you study this book carefully, you'll see that it's the only step! For the second step, you'll have to buy a second copy of this book. (You just received Lesson Number 1—people who write, illustrate, edit, print and distribute these silly Mad paperback books are among the most cunning and devious of your enemies, financially speaking.) But let us continue ...

We have separated the enemies, not according to types, like Mother, Father, Brother, Teacher, etc, but by how they act! In this way, you'll be able to spot them more easily. What you do about them once you've spotted them is your problem!

ANXIETY

Just what is "Anxiety"? And who the hell cares? Well, since we have to talk about something for 192 pages, why not talk about "Anxiety"?

Let's put it this way: If we got all upset worrying that you didn't know the meaning of Anxiety, we'd have Anxiety—and that's one thing we don't need. (Did you buy that extra copy yet? Don't put it off, we're warning you!) Since we're not worried about whether or not you know what Anxiety is, then we don't have Anxiety. Confused? Why not! What else do you have to do? Chances are you're a kid and nobody cares about you, anyway! But, if your parents get Anxiety attacks, you're in big trouble!

Like this...

If your mother is the *anxious* type (anxious; ie: one who has anxiety, dummy!), then make sure she *never* accompanies you to your Little League games! She believes it's just a matter of time before you receive a mortal injury while playing...

A father is also subject to anxiety attacks! Like the father who keeps peeking into your room because he's worried if you're sleeping or not. And if you *are* sleeping, then he worries if you're *breathing* or not!

A teacher's anxiety is something you have to watch out for. However, there doesn't seem to be any defense against the old bat who wants to help you 'realize your full potential.' Her anxiety is one of your *deadliest* enemies and is responsible for killing even more weekends than parents who argue ...

Divorced parents seem to have a lot of anxiety that they *dump* on their kids without the slightest hesitation. This is understandable, since neither Mommy nor Daddy have each other to dump on anymore...

I want you to promise Daddy that you won't tell Mommy about his new *sportscar!*

We promise!

On your doggie's life!

There are anxieties that an *older sister* has that will make your life miserable, especially at the dinner table. When she gets afraid she is putting on an extra ounce, the family rallies to "Give her support" and goes on a diet with her. At that point, food becomes just a fond memory. This is one of the many reasons for considering your older sister among your most dreaded enemies...

Your own anxiety can often be an enemy! By worrying too much about what might happen, surprising things sometimes do and do not happen...

OVERPROTECTIVENESS

Parents in all parts of the animal kingdom protect their young. In the human family, this protection is usually carried to extremes. Even though your mother and father may look like gorillas, you would be better off it they acted more like them! 'Overprotectiveness' is an enemy despite the fact that it is usually disguised as "Tender, Loving Care." Don't fall for it!

The Overprotective Parent is only really happy when she thinks her offspring is protected against the elements...

The Overprotective Parent comes by her craziness naturally. She inherited it from her mother. Grandmothers often take on the coloration of the enemy by being even more Overprotective than Mothers...

Because most fathers are blithering idiots when it comes to questions about health, they freak out and become Overprotective instantly—no matter how *trivial* the cause! They are enemies because they drive you nuts with their concern which is composed of 55% ignorance and 45% guilt...

How bad is it?

He has 99.2.

Oh God, spare him, spare him, spare him, spare him!

COMICS

The OP (Overprotective) mother is a particular burden for the teenage girl to bear. The OP (see above) mother takes all her fears and transfers them to the daughter. Even though the OP (see above) mother can't put her own life together, she has no doubts that she can manage her daughter's if only the girl would listen to her and do everything the old goof wants her to do...

However, there is a *brighter side* to handling the OP! If you play your cards right, you can get the enemy to use her craziness to *your* advantage! Sometimes you can win more by *surrendering* than by *fighting* to the bitter end ...

NEGATIVISM

From the high-toned sound of this category, you might think that this is something good! But you don't know anything! Negativism is not a philosophy, it's the attitude of a perpetual grouch, which is exactly what most of your parents are turning out to be, right? But with a kid like you, who can blame them? But that's another story! (Better get over to the bookstore—these books are going like hotcakes and you don't want to be left out in the cold, do you?) Okay, now that you've returned from the bookstore with your dozen extra copies, we'll continue...

You might say, "Who cares about stuff like that?" Ha! It's just that kind of question that shows how much you need this book! Your parents' negative attitude victimizes you in many ways, some not so subtle and others not so subtle (Went right over that, did you? No wonder your Reading Comprehension Score stinks!)

Remember this: your parents', teachers', and relatives' negativism will get you in the end! Let us show you in pictures, which is probably your natural mode of reading...

The Negative Mother is so sure that something *terrible* is about to happen, that when it doesn't, she gets confused and breaks out in illogical, foolish statements. And if you're anywhere nearby, guess who gets the abuse?

Most of our fathers are negative (have you seen what most of our mothers look like early in the morning?). It's a good idea to avoid them at least for the first twenty-one years of your life…

We had a good time in school today…

One attribute of the N.M. (Negative Mother) is her willingness to make predictions for which she has absolutely no substantiation. In other words...naw, those words are good enough—*look 'em up* if you're stumped!

If you took some pride in your appearance, maybe some boy would take you out instead of you spending Saturday Nights alone.

Being *alone*, I can handle! It's being alone with *you* that's impossible to take!

Negativism can be catching. If one of your friends has an N.P. (Negative Parent), chances are he will be an N.F. (Negative Friend). Find a place on your enemy list for *this* bird! He's sure to make you feel *rotten*, sooner or later...

Unfortunately, you run the risk of becoming a Negative Guy (N.G.) *yourself!* Then you become your *own* enemy, and who do you talk to about *that?* How can you avoid becoming an N.G.? Keep as far away as possible from poltroons like "Funny Uncles."

This Whoopie Cushion'll kill them!

Are you sure?

Guaranteed! They'll *die!*

PARENTAL PARTICIPATION

So you complain that your folks have no interest in you or what you do, huh? Well, maybe that's not the worst thing in the world! Maybe if they did have an interest in everything you did, that might be the worst thing in the world! What are we trying to say? Simply this: high on the list of enemies are the parents, relatives and other old fogies who want to participate in your life and grab off some of the goodies for themselves ...

The mother who participates in her kid's life doesn't stop when mealtime comes around! The dinner bell is her signal to really swing into action ...

Be sure you give that *forty chews!*

Can I give it just twenty? It's *soup!*

Friends of the family are usually no friends of yours. Because they knew you when you were "just a tot" they think that they have a right to horn in on your life! Is this the action of a *friend* or an *enemy*? Are these questions too *tough* for you? Would you like to lie down with a cold compress over your forehead? Don't you wish it was Friday? Damn it, says *something*!

Do you take this woman to be …

… of course he does—even though he's not nearly good enough for her!

There doesn't seem to be any remedy known to modern science that can stop an out-of-shape father from trying to convince his kids that he was once a great ball player! This kind of parental participation can be lethal for you if the old fool is trying to pitch to you; lethal for him if he tries to play the outfield ...

Relatives really believe that you are born without any *rights* at all! They can barge right into your life and actually think you should *thank* them for it! Watch out for relatives who "take an interest" in you...

Know what you should study in college? *Gene splicing!* *That's* where the big money's gonna be in the future!

I'd like to splice our family's genes and throw his half away!

ANGER

"Anger"—now there's an attitude for you! Actually, it's such a lousy attitude that it gets us angry just thinking about it. We don't mean that your anger is a bad thing. Nooooooo! After all, to anger is human, but not always. When your parents get angry, then it's a different story altogether! No matter how uninvolved you think you may be, you're going to get the smeary end of the stick! So remember this, young person: whenever either of your parents, or both of your parents get angry, try to be somewhere else! Otherwise you are looking right down the throat of the enemy...

Take a look! This kid obviously didn't read *this* book! He is upset that his folks are fighting. What the hell did he think folks did all the time—make love? They're *married,* dummy!

One of the problems with having parents who get angry is that they serve as "role models" for older brothers and sisters. To these fledgling irascibles (*another* word to look up someday when you get a chance or when you get to be thirty-five years old, whichever comes first!)

A good idea is to try and block the sound of your parents' voices. This can be done in one of two ways. One, the hard way: shoot off a cannon whenever they start yelling at you! This is not only expensive, but it is probably not loud enough to drown out their sound. The second way is to clamp on your stereo headset fast and turn the volume up to the "Extreme Pain" setting! Of course this may impair your hearing. But after all, what you're hearing at home isn't worth hearing, anyway!

Let's face it, divorced mothers have it *tough!* And we understand how they can get angry from time to time. However, even if she is your mother, her anger is still *her* business pal, not yours! Also, the guy she's probably steamed up about is your old flesh and blood *poppa!* So, there's nothing you can do when the old lady gets really T'd, because sooner or later *you* are going to remind her of the old man! Get it?

No alimony check? I'm going to have that rat *thrown in jail!*

Please don't say things like that ...

EMBARRASSMENT

One of the greatest enemies of young people is Embarrassment, or what is also commonly known as Shame! When your parents embarrass you, life loses its meaning and death its sting! You know what we're talking about...

It's not easy for a divorced mother to meet new guys, so she has to use techniques that can be a source of great embarrassment to her children...

How in the world did you ever get my phone number?

It's on phone booths all over town—in *your* handwriting!

When one of your parents embarrasses you, it's mighty tough to take. But when *both* parents do it to you, where do you go to hide?

Even though a parent's absence can cause embarrassment, their presence can cause even *more* pain...

Little brothers are bundles of potential embarrassment just waiting to explode...

NATURE

As goofy little kids, we were taught that Mother Nature is kindly, loving and dear. Oh yeah? Ask the rabbit who gets swooped up in the eagle's talons! Check with the zebra who becomes the lion's brunch! Or have a heart-to-heart chat with the fly who has to spend his lifetime tap-dancing on dog doo! Yicch!

Now what has this to do with you? Nothing, so go out and have a soda! Of course, if you do, you run the risk of the rest of us talking about you! And wouldn't you just love to know what we said? Ah ha, you're not as dumb as you look—you're staying! Okay, so listen ...

Nature is an enemy of yours! In fact, we're going to demonstrate it to you in pictures and text. The pictures you can probably understand without aid! If you must, ask a friend to read the text to you ...

Mother Nature has a lot of surprises in store for *little* boys as they grow to be *big* boys! With these surprises come various *rituals* that are observed by most teenage boys. So, if you have an older brother who takes five showers a day, just chalk it up as one of Mother Nature's little shockers! But you're the one in for the shock...

Mother Nature sometimes plays dirty little pranks on people, especially older divorced men. Mama N. lets them think they are young again and can date women half their age. Unfortunately these old Swingers don't realize that their own *daughters* are half their age, too! Daughters of divorced men, *beware!* Mother Nature is about to make a schmuck out of your father! And anyone who would do that to the old fool, certainly qualifies as an enemy of the family...

I'm sure you will have a lot in *common* with Trudy...

No doubt a lot more than *you* have!

One of the lousy things about Mother Nature is that she takes such a *long time* to do what she has to do. For instance, she seems to be dawdling when it comes to maturing your younger brother! How long will Mother N. permit him to be a lower form of *animal* before allowing him into the family of man? How long must you endure the deathly embarrassments he deals out, daily? *Too long,* that's how long!

Mother Nature has a sense of humor. Unfortunately, it's a lot like the sense of humor the Marquis De Sade had! The old crone must really think that bestowing zits on the human race was a dilly of a joke! Unfortunately her funny bone needs work. When you're old enough to think about *girls*, then you're old enough to think about your face breaking out and looking like some action painting by Jackson Pollack (ask around)! It is in the field of *Zitology* that Mother Nature shows what a cruel enemy she can be...

A while back we said a few unkind words about older men who go out with much younger women. But how about older *women* who go out with much younger men? How about that, we ask! Also, how do we get in on the action, we also ask! Anyway, the older woman/younger man syndrome is no less nor more attractive than the older man/younger woman syndrome! You know something, we're beginning to lose interest in the whole damn thing.

However, to finish it off; Mother Nature not only makes Love blind, she also makes Love dopey when it comes to large age disparities...

NON SEQUITURS

We know that understanding English is diffi-
cult enough for most of you out there. So when a
Latin phrase is used, we can imagine how your
faces glaze over and sleep granules form in the
corners of your mean little eyes!

Okay, so maybe you will learn something by
reading this! Like—what is a "Non Sequitur"? An
obscure Christian holy day? Nope! Well then, is it
something you suck on when you have a chest
cold? Closer, but still no! Well, what then?

A "Non Sequitur" is a statement that doesn't
follow what was said or done before! In other
words, "Xaeandu plesaava dun" (the other words
in this case being an obscure Indonesian dialect
known to only two people, one of whom is dead).
Let's put it this way: It is an inappropriate remark!
Or put this way: It is an inappropriate remark!

Parents are experts when it comes to "Non
Sequiturs!" And you know that anything they're
good at is a potential threat to you! A "Non Sequitur" is a powerful enemy weapon. Study this section. It will do more good, although give you less
pleasure, than touching yourself in forbidden
places...

Non sequiturs have a tendency to come tumbling out when Mothers are emotionally upset and vulnerable, which is most of their waking hours! But to be fair to parents, they... aw, the hell with that! If you wanted to be fair to parents, you wouldn't have bought this book in the first place! Read on...

I just got run over by a steamroller!

Fathers break out in Non sequiturs when they encounter anything they don't understand! That's a lot of non sequiturs, true! Instead of trying to understand, fathers have the unlovely habit of immediately surrendering to the irrational ...

Most parents are not capable of fast, witty or even sensible reponses to a child's question! Therefore, they have invented the *non sequitur!* The confusing thing about non sequiturs is that parents say them with as much conviction as they would say things that made *sense!* So, kids, here's a tip. Forget how the old windbags express themselves and pay attention to what they *actually say!* If they don't make *sense,* you know your parents are taking refuge in the last bastion of the idiot—the *non sequitur!*

INVASION OF PRIVACY

Want to get really upset? Think of the last time that your parents or your brothers or sisters invaded your privacy. See, we told you you'd get upset! Invasion of privacy is one of the worse things in the world! It's a lot worse than the invasion of Afghanistan. (After all, do you know somebody who lives in Afghanistan?)

Anyway, your privacy probably resides on the bottom of your parents' priority list! Sometimes one feels that a parent invented privacy in the first place so it could be invaded by another parent in the second place!

Enough talk, it's time for action! Read now ...

Teenagers are particularly sensitive to invasions of their privacy. That's because they do so many shameful and dirty things they don't want anyone to find out about! Hold it! We're just kidding, just kidding. (Teenagers also have rotten senses of humor!). To counteract your parents' nosiness, hit 'em with a smart aleck response when they start prying! It might not end their nasty habit, but if it makes their lives a little more *miserable*, at least you've accomplished *something!*

Telephones are nothing less than magical in the way they stimulate an otherwise indifferent mother's interest in her daughter's activities!

Take heed, teenager. If there is an extension phone in your house, your conversations become *public domain!* Therefore, it's best to do your phoning *outside* from a phone booth and hope that your mother isn't perched up a nearby telephone pole tapping the phone line!

Tell him if he doesn't take you to the prom, you'll never speak to him again!

That won't work! He might think I said that *you'll* never speak to him again!

When parents get divorced they undergo many peculiar changes. Not the least is changing from people who were totally uninterested in each other when they were married to being very interested in each other as soon as they're apart! This doesn't sound too bad? Really? Well, guess who's smack in the middle *between* them? *You,* that's who! You are now the *confidential agent* for both of them, expected to snitch on your mother to your father and vice versa! So *you* actually become the one who is invading your parents' privacy!

There are two things that little brothers simply do not know. One is *shame* and the other is respect for your privacy! Since little brothers are headed towards the penitentiary anyhow, they might as well get an early start in their crime careers by sneaking into your room and going through your valuable possessions! Once they come upon your diary, they have hit the jackpot! Your life, dear older sister, is now *over!*

Once your little brother reads your innermost thoughts and feelings, the only course left for you is to become a heart transplant donor!

Parties give meddlers wonderful opportunities to invade your privacy! Not only do these unwanted intruders make you uncomfortable, but they also make you look like a total schmuck in front of your friends! But we shouldn't be uncharitable—your parents are entitled to *some fun* out of life! After all, look who they're *married* to!

CHEAPNESS

This heading is self explanatory—especially if you didn't buy extra copies of this book, like we asked you! But your own cheapness isn't the only thing that makes your life so empty! It's the cheapness of others that is the real enemy! Why, you may ask, are people cheap? To which we answer, forget it! We're not about to turn this otherwise hilarious book into some kind of psychology text! Now, be good, stop asking questions, and read...

One thing is for sure—fathers head the cheapness list! For instance, they're really bonkers about *electricity!* They have a passion for turning off lights to save a dime's worth of juice! To them, it's a big deal!

Cheapness can be *hereditary!* Sometimes your little sister might inherit it from your father! Then you're *surrounded!* So you'd better *quit school* and get a job or else money may become something you once *heard* about! Little sisters are a *mean bunch* to begin with, and when you want something from *them*—especially something of *value*—you have a better chance of building a *snowman* on the *Equator!*

At times even your best friends can be afflicted with sudden attacks of cheapness. These attacks usually occur when they are called upon to pay their fair share of something, like *tolls!* Then your friends become subject to the well known virus, *Toll Boothus Sleepus,* which renders them *unconscious* until after *you* have paid the toll! Then, as if by magic, they awaken!

INCONSISTENCY

Here's a beauty for you! It's the natural inclination of parents to be inconsistent. "How does this manifest itself," you ask? Do you always ask so many questions?, we ask! Okay, if you stop asking, we'll stop asking! Anyway, where were we…oh, yeah—Inconsistency…

Mothers are, by *nature,* inconsistent. Don't ask why—it's just how it is. Unfortunately, their inconsistency is not improved by divorce. (Not much else is improved by divorce either, when you come to think of it!) For when Mommy goes back to dating, her mind is in a constant state of conflict, and that leads to *more* Inconsistency.

You're going to have a *wonderful time* sleeping over at Billy's house tonight...

But I don't want to!

Who *asked* you?

Ever hear of *Dr. Jekyll* and *Mr. Hyde*? Now *there* was world class inconsistency for you! You may *think* that no one is really like that—*nice* one minute and *awful* the next! You may think that, but remember: *You're* just a dopey kid who wastes good money on crummy books like these! So what the hell do *you* know? Look around if you want to see people as inconsistent as Dr. "J" and Mr. "H…"

No *wonder* you kids are rotten— you're just like your *father*!

When it comes to *clothing styles,* parents make no sense at all! Did you ever notice how *quick* they are to condemn the newest teenage fashions? They are only faster at doing one other thing—adopting those same teenage fashions!

Here's a bit of *bad news* for you! Sorry that we have to be the ones to tell you, but as you grow up you will take on many of the characteristics of those ogres known as your parents! This is no laughing matter! *You* will find that you do a lot of things just like *they* do, think a lot like *they* think, and even use the same cliches *they* use! Life *stinks*, doesn't it? Anyway, according to this immutable (another gem for you, free) law, teenage girls will act like their old ladies in many ways. One way is in being totally inconsistent about their appearance...

VANITY

Do you know that Vanity is one of the Seven Deadly Sins? Well, It is! "So what!" you say? Maybe you got too much to say, kiddo! Maybe you should shut up for a while and learn something! You think this intro is hostile? Well, what happened when we were nice and lovely and begged you to get additional copies of this book? Did you run out and get them? Ha! So why should we be nice to you?

Vanity? Oh, yeah—Let's see how other people's vanity can affect you! (Meanwhile, we'll look into our heart and try to forgive you for being such an inconsiderate person!)

There are *two things* that your mother—assuming she's a normal mother—*can't stand*! One of them is growing *older*! The other is *you*! Not being able to stand *you* is understandable! We can't either! However, not being able to *grow older* could use a little examining! Women feel they were not designed by The Almighty to grow older! That only happens to men and crones in Fairy Tales, but not them! sorry, Mom...

Vanity does affect some men, too! For instance, *divorced men*! Divorced men are like the women they left—they don't think that Father Time has his eye on *them* either! *Wrong*! Perhaps the divorced father is even *more* ridiculous than his ex! He thinks because he still has a few wisps of hair left, he's a *young buck*! Unfortunately, he forgets what happens to bucks in *hunting season...*

Now what do you say we try and be *nice* to our folks for a moment, huh? It's just a *moment*, for gosh sakes! It won't *kill you!*

Many mothers, as they get older, want to change their appearances via *plastic surgery!* So what's *wrong* with that? Look at it this way—When *you* get up in the morning and glance in the mirror, you see *you!* Not *good*, but not *too* bad! Think what *your poor mother* sees when *she* looks in the mirror in the morning! What can she do about it, get a *new mirror*? So if Mommy decides to have her *face fixed*, don't give her a *hard time*, hear?

That's the *last* kind thing we'll say about parents in this book! Promise!

Mommy's going to have a *face lift!*

The doctor'll have to use a *derrick!*

SELF-PITY

Self-Pity is bad enough when you have it, but when your parents have it—take a walk and don't come back! "Why?" Again the questions! Because they get real dramatic and give tear-jerking performances ranging from Soap Opera to Grand Opera! That's why! But don't be taken in or start feeling sorry for them! They can do that much better than you can! A better idea is to straighten them up with a well placed zinger or two, like ...

Fathers seem to have a very low resistance to Self-Pity attacks! They can be hurt in *so many ways* that it makes no sense to list them *all* here! These self inflicted wounds are just that—self-inflicted! They should be left alone to heal by themselves!

When I was your age, I never would have chosen to do my *homework* rather than playing "Catch" with my dad!

If you had, mabe you'd be a *smarter* adult today!

Take a look! Is this an acting class we're watching? Is this woman reacting to news that the world is coming to an end? Has she suddenly lost her mind? Well, the answers to the above questions are No; No; and Yes! She is doing her self-pity shtick...

For someone with a large dose of Self-Pity there's nothing better than a *psychiatrist*! Not that a psychiatrist will cure such a person, but who else would sit and listen to all that Self-Pitying stuff? (Anyone who'd sit and listen to that stuff should have his *own* head examined!) However, Self-Pity people use their shrink sessions to rehearse for their home performances...

I'm having such a bad day, I'm seriously considering killing myself...

But you're not finished with your psychotherapy yet! When you are, *then* you can consider doing it!

The worst thing you can do to people who are bathing in Self-Pity is to try and help them get rid of the *"bath water."* In other words, do *not* try to make those people feel *better*! The pure, unvarnished truth of the matter is, THEY DO NOT WANT TO FEEL BETTER! They're having a *wonderful time* feeling bad! "Wrong," *you* say? Wanna bet? *we* say! So, unless you're willing to put your *money* where your mouth is, button your lip and *learn* something, clod!

Parents are good at Self-Pity, but *teenage girls* have elevated this attitude to an *art form*! Teenage girls have the advantage of their youth over their experience! In short, *they* can have a good tantrum when they are afflicted with a Self-Pity fit, whereas their *parents* can't! (Actually parents *could*, but they'd be thrown into padded rooms!)

More on teenage girls and Self-Pity! (They're such easy targets!) If a young lady doesn't have at least *one* life-threatening crisis a day, she just hasn't gotten the hang of being a teenager! Here's the recipe: Take one small incident, add a large dose of emotionalism, sprinkle in a *soupçon* (hoo ha) of perceived injustice and stir until ready. With *your* parents, the opportunity to serve this malodorous concoction will come soon enough—be patient!

What do you mean I can't go away overnight with some friends? You're ruining my entire life!

Impossible! Don't you remember, we ruined your life *last week* when we said you had to clean your room before you went to the movies?

EXPECTATIONS

This one's a real killer! As a kid you can't be blamed for being chock-full of expectations! After all, what do you know about the world or how it works? Kids expect that great things are in the future, just waiting to happen! That's sweet! But stupid!

Learn this and learn it well—Expectations are made to be unfulfilled, especially if your parents are involved! If they promise you something, bet the farm that you will be disappointed when that promise is kept! That's assuming that the promise is kept! (Parents know only so many things, but one thing the have down pat is how to weasel out of promises they make to you! Ever notice that? We're friends, we can talk!)

To help parents counteract *Expectations*, a thing called "Work" was invented! This convenience gets fathers out of doing what they promised they would do for their kids, while making them seem like heroes! When what *you* want collides with what one of *your parents* wants, guess *who* loses? Need a hint?

The *divorced father* is usually delighted to see his offspring! And why not? He only sees them for a couple of hours each week, while leaving the *old bag* to put up with them the rest of the time! But even with only a few hours at his disposal, the old man can find ways of defeating his children's fondest expectations...

Now, aside from broken promises, are there other ways in which *Expectations* can be unfulfilled? Good question! Glad *we* asked it and not *you* with your *dumb* questions! Where were we ... oh, yeah ... sometimes people who are totally *unaware* of your desires can frustrate you! Like the pretty girl who lives in the next house! She probably doesn't know of your interest in her! (Lucky for you, or her folks would cripple you!)

Come on, come on—leave the shades up! Please! Nobody's *watching* you ... not even me ... I'm just *appreciating* you!

SELF INVOLVEMENT

Isn't it a shame the way some people only think about <u>themselves</u>? Like youngsters who won't help out a friend by buying additional copies of his wonderful book? But let's not get into that! You know who you are, out there! Anyway...

When people become <u>Self Involved</u>, the world could stop spinning and they wouldn't <u>notice</u>! Now, if you've read <u>this</u> far, you should be able to guess to whom we are referring. ("To whom"? A grammatical construction that would <u>thrill</u> your old English teacher! And she probably could <u>use</u> one! We move on...). That's right, kiddies, your <u>parents</u> are prime candidates for The <u>Olympic Self Involvement Team</u>! Examples are herewith set forth...

Dear old Dad has <u>plenty</u> of room in his head! Unfortunately it won't be filled with anything but his <u>own</u> concerns...

In an <u>emergency</u> you can usually depend on your parents—to do the <u>wrong</u> thing or be in the <u>wrong</u> place! So much for dependability! Why should this be so? Because they're too involved with <u>themselves</u> to be of much use to <u>anyone else</u>! Take this good advice—become <u>self-sufficient</u> as soon as you can! Then <u>you</u> can become as <u>Self Involved</u> as <u>they</u> are!

Self Involvement has a sub division known as "Possessiveness" which is merely Self Involvement stretched to include "things." "Things" are very important to your parents! Without "things," they wouldn't know why they work at jobs they hate! "Things" are also deeply symbolic and highly charged emotionally for them! Beware! When you start messing in those areas, everything gets very goofy …

The next example never really happens, but it <u>reads</u> funny! Actually, it's not <u>too</u> far from the truth, since some older people really feel they are the center of the universe and are of universal concern...

What's the matter, Dad?

What do you think they're talking about in that huddle? **Me**, that's what!

One of the most obvious symptoms of <u>Self Involvement</u> is "Hypochondria" or—for the <u>mono-syllabic</u> slobs among us—people who <u>believe</u> they are sick when they're <u>not</u>!

BULL

This section is unique! "Why?" How many chapter titles have you seen that are only half a word! But enough of that, time grows short! (Hey, wouldn't this be a good opportunity to race out and buy the extra copies of this book that you've promised yourself? We'll wait for you...

...) See, you didn't miss __anything__ while you were gone!

Where were we? Oh yes! This section deals with the con jobs, evasions, and downright <u>bull-whatever</u> people dump on you! Now we're not talking about people who don't <u>matter</u> to you! We're talking <u>relationships</u>, buster! Heck, if someone who <u>doesn't</u> mean much unloads a wagonfull of steamy stuff on you, who cares? But when parents, friends and even people you <u>like</u> do it, then it <u>smarts</u>!

People lie because it's easier than telling the truth! Like the <u>last sentence</u>, for instance! Saying what we did is a lot easier than having to think about a <u>good</u> answer, or worse, doing <u>research</u> on the subject! Come to think of it, the previous statement, just like the one you're reading now, is <u>also</u> a lie! I think we'd better get on with it ...

Because it's an area from which you're excluded, your Dad's business world is cloaked in mystery and only revealed via the bull he chooses to talk about! Actually, his business world is as meaningless as your little world! And you know how meaningless <u>that</u> is! Here's some free advice: Don't feel too sorry for Dear Old Dad when he claims to be burdened with business matters ...

I hope you have a good time, Daddy!

Good time? You think these business conventions are **fun?** It's strictly **business** all day long!

I hope you didn't forget to pack your noise makers and water balloons!

The Divorced mother has special problems, especially when it comes to <u>dating</u>! For some reason, she is usually embarrassed when a new date shows up! Is she embarrassed because you see <u>him</u> or because he sees <u>you</u>? Let's assume that it's because you see <u>him</u> (not a totally safe assumption by any means)! When this happens, Mommy must "<u>Pretend</u>," which is just a pre-school way of saying, "<u>Lie!</u>"

Divorced fathers <u>also</u> have their problems. Unfortunately, all too often <u>their</u> problems become <u>your</u> problems...

I'm getting killed with debts, Your Honor! Look at these bills! One from a hotel in The Bahamas for me and my secretary; this one for my beach club membership; my hair transplant; my dancing lessons and my new Porsche! Thousands of dollars, just for the bare **necessities** of life! And my ex-wife wants me to give her **more** money! Can you imagine such **insensitivity?**

Teenage boys will use <u>anything</u> to get what they want, sexually speaking! Because the urge in teenage boys is so overwhelming, they sometimes <u>forget</u> that the girls they are trying to mess with have <u>brains</u>, too! But, come to think of it, it's not their <u>brains</u> that teenage boys want to fool around with, is it?

Your bra strap is cutting off your **circulation**! I'll just undo it! You wouldn't want to get **gangrene**, would you?

Take a walk! Last week, you told me that soul kissing prevented **Leprosy**!

Everyone likes to be thought of as having all the <u>virtues</u>! However, very few of us like to pay the price for <u>earning</u> those virtues! <u>Uncles</u> fit this category comfortably ...

TATTLING

Science has yet to answer the main question about younger brothers and sisters! That question is, "<u>Who needs them?</u>" What possible function these people have is impossible to determine! After all, science can only explain so much! We will also have to wait for research to give us a clue as to why <u>younger</u> brothers and sisters have an insatiable desire to tattle on <u>older</u> brothers and sisters!

Little brothers and sisters have so little to enjoy! They can barely read, they can't think very well, and their bodies are no fun at all yet! So they must look for other things to entertain them! And one of the closest things at hand is you! Aren't you glad you furnish so much merriment for the little angels?

Never try to be suave, cool or anything other than absent when little siblings are around! They will <u>foul up</u> your act, sure as you're born (which is more than you can say about them)!

A question for you to ponder—why do parents <u>always</u> believe the little rat when he/she tattles on you? Perhaps it's because it's more comforting to think of <u>you</u> as a terrible person than to think of your <u>sibling</u> as a liar! After all, they <u>already</u> believe they have one liar in the family—<u>you</u>! Sound right to you? No? Then forget it!

THE DOUBLE STANDARD

We just took a look at siblings who <u>tattled</u> on their older brothers and sisters! That was bad enough! But there's something that the little creeps are involved in that's even <u>harder</u> to take! The <u>Double Standard</u>. What is the <u>D.S.</u>? It's when there's one set of rules that <u>you</u> have to live by and another for them! It's enough to make you want to leave home—or to search for a roving caravan that might want to <u>buy</u> your sibling!

Just why parents think that younger brothers and sisters need their <u>protection</u> is a mystery we will never solve! The little imps have a survival instinct rivalled only by that of the <u>cockroach</u>! (And the similarity doesn't end there, but that's <u>another</u> matter!)

When the situations are <u>reversed</u>, do your parents take <u>your</u> side? Are you kidding? Hah! and "hah" again!

ADVICE

Beware the <u>advice giver</u>. It's usually an aunt whose only exercise is sticking her nose into your business! These people are to be avoided at all cost! For some reason, your parents will believe them while doubting themselves! "Why is that?" What is this—a philosophy book? <u>Cheese, Louise!</u>

INSECURITY

It's not easy discussing <u>insecurity</u>! Tell you why. If you're <u>already</u> insecure, this section will make you even more so! If you're <u>not</u> insecure, reading this section will make you insecure! What can you do about it? Simple. Don't read this! You already have, you say? Well, that's what you get for reading things you shouldn't! Anyway, it's bad enough when <u>you're</u> insecure, but when your <u>parents</u> are insecure, there's nothing you can do about it! Okay? Resume reading ...

How does a father's insecurity victimize his young? Well, for one thing, you never know if he <u>means</u> it when he says <u>"Yes"</u> to something! It's like having a wet noodle for a father! How's that for a <u>role model</u>, pasta fans?

People with insecurities often have little <u>annoying habits</u>! Picking one's nose is among the <u>most</u> annoying of these habits! Why do insecure people pick their noses? We don't know! But that's only because we don't want to spend any time <u>thinking about it</u>! However, if that subject appeals to you, then by all means, think about it! And after you get done thinking about that—forget it ... we're getting ill!

THINGS THAT GO "BUMP" IN YOUR LIFE

Isn't that an <u>intriguing title</u> for a chapter in this wonderful book? Of course, but what does it mean? It means that there are not only PEOPLE but also THINGS that are your natural enemies!

To be fully equipped for the <u>terrible struggles</u> you will have in the future, you had better commit this section to <u>memory</u>! And to insure that this explosive information doesn't get into the hands of your <u>other</u> enemies, we suggest you <u>eat this</u> page —then throw your <u>head</u> away!

"SCHOOL HOT LUNCHES"

There are no more revolting sights than what drops on your plate in the school cafeteria! Oh, yes, there is a more revolting sight—watching how they <u>prepare</u> the slop in the <u>kitchen</u>! School cooks have to pass a Civil Service exam before they can get the job! Unfortunately, it's the <u>same test</u> given for <u>sewer workers</u>...

I'd better eat this **fast!** It's starting to **advance** on me!

"THE EGO-DESTROYING GYM HORSE"

If gym class does one thing best, it's exposing your weaknesses and holding them up to ridicule! That's where you're reduced from a 97 lb. weakling to a 97 lb. pile of raw sewage! And the instrument used to degrade you is called, "The Gym Horse!"

Some people are adept at the intricacies of Gym Horse exercises, but they can do something that you probably have not mastered yet—being able to get up on the damn thing in the first place!

"THE HOME MOVIE MENACE"

If your parents have a <u>movie camera</u>, realize that you will be in for some <u>rough times!</u> They will insist on showing embarrassing home movies of you when you a dopey bare-bottomed kid who didn't know enough to take cover! However, if you have enough guts, you might be able to stop this parental monkey shine with a well placed <u>moon shine</u>...

Hey, if you folks are so interested, let me show you what it looks like now!

"THE LOOSE LOOSE LEAF PAGES"

Who invented the <u>loose leaf book</u>? We know one thing—he was a sadist! No matter how hard you try, loose leaf pages will fall out! Not <u>all</u> the pages, just the <u>important</u> ones! It's not an accident! The evil genius who devised the loose leaf book <u>planned</u> it that way...

"THE SAVE-A-SEAT SUICIDE"

If anyone ever asks you to save his seat while he goes out for popcorn or soda—do not do it! Suppose you're saving a seat and a <u>big guy</u> wants to take it! You have a choice—either you can <u>lose a friend</u> or you can <u>lose your teeth</u>! Since you can always get more friends, let the seat go to the roughest bidder! However, there may be a way around this, but you need <u>courage</u> to lie to someone <u>twice</u> your size...

I just **threw up** on this seat!

"THE DEADLY TERM READING LIST"

Wouldn't it be nice to be able to foretell the future? Well, you can in one area—your English Class! Because when you get the term reading list and see such titles as "Silas Marner," "As You Like It," and "David Copperfield," you can safely predict that for the next six months you're going to spend a lot of time being <u>bored</u> out of your <u>gourd</u>...

"THE GHASTLY GAS STATION REST ROOM"

One of the <u>least</u> pleasant things about travelling is the dreaded <u>Gas Station toilet</u>! Thinking about it is enough to make one want to cancel his trip! Here's a thought for you—suppose those places aren't <u>really</u> toilets after all, but are actually <u>secret laboratories</u> used by scientists to discover and examine every germ and disease that is known to man! Not very <u>probable</u>, you say? Maybe not, but then again, what could be more improbable than those horrible little toilets?

"THE EVIL SMELLING EGG SALAD SANDWICH"

If your mother does not have time to fix your lunch and volunteers to make you a quick <u>egg salad sandwich</u>, DO NOT LET HER DO IT! Do you have any idea what a warm egg salad sandwich smells like to people on a <u>crowded bus</u>! Do you have any idea what people on a crowded bus might do to someone they think is emitting such odors? And finally, where do you want your body shipped? It is far better to go <u>hungry</u> than to face certain death so early in the morning...

"THE CAPRICIOUS COPIER"

Not only can a malfunctioning copier machine chew up your hard work and spit it out at you in no sensible order, but it can instill a death wish in you that might <u>never</u> go away! You have grown up depending on machines to work for you! Trusting soul, poor trusting soul! What you don't seem to know is that machines are always ready to rebel and shake off their <u>slave status</u>! And when is the best time for such a rebellion? When the stakes are <u>highest</u>! So next time you want to have a term paper or a college application or your birth certificate copied, the machine is going to <u>louse you up</u>! Bet on it!

"THE TOILET PAPER CAPER"

And while we're on the subject, if you're familiar with the expression, "Act in haste, repent in leisure," you're sure to understand it much better after you've raced into a bathroom without first checking to make sure there was <u>toilet paper</u>! Life holds few more embarrassing moments, especially if you're in a girlfriend or boyfriend's home! What can you do? Perhaps the best advice is to remove the empty toilet paper tube and use it as a megaphone to announce to the outside world that you are going to commit <u>suicide</u>! This may not be the <u>only</u> way to handle the situation! However, it is the <u>best</u> way ...

"THE INSCRUTABLE INSTRUCTION SHEET"

Try, just try to assemble anything that requires an <u>instruction sheet</u> and it's even money that your sanity will never be the same! That's because Instruction Sheets are not written to be <u>understood</u>! In comparison to the instructions for assembling the simplest toy, "The Mysteries Of The Cabala" is kids' stuff! Just remember, when you hear the words, "<u>Some assembly required</u>," that that particular item is not for you! We can't prove that writing indecipherable instructions is a <u>Russian plot</u>! On the other hand, we can't prove that it <u>isn't</u>!

"THE MESS ON THE MOVIE FLOOR"

Ever try to walk through a row in the movies quickly so you won't disturb the others who are watching the film? Take it from us, it <u>can't</u> be done! Why? Because there is so much <u>goo</u> on the floor from spilled Cokes, old chewing gum and melted candy that it would be easier running The 100 Yard Dash in deep sea divers' boots! Some people never make it to the aisle and have to be buried right in the theater! That may explain the <u>unidentified smell</u> in many movie houses...

"THE COSTLY COKE MACHINE"

Don't you smack your lips when you see an ice cold Coke pouring into a cup? But what do you smack when you see the ice cold Coke pouring and there isn't any <u>cup</u> for it to pour into? You try <u>smacking</u> the <u>machine</u>! Unfortunately, that does no good! Perhaps if you smacked the <u>manager</u>... Naw, he'd probably beat your brains out! (Our research indicates that kids who buy these Mad Paperback Books are usually small, weak and unable to defend themselves!)

"WARRANTIES YOU CAN NEITHER UNDERSTAND NOR READ"

My, but doesn't the word "Warranty" sound official and good? It's as if some big company is standing behind its product proudly, dependably, almost Godlike in its honesty. Makes you want to either pray or salute (depending upon whether you're in school or not). However, if you try to read the warranty, you'll soon find you are learning a <u>second language!</u> The language of the warranty is an <u>enemy</u>—it makes you <u>think</u> you're being protected when you're really being <u>shafted</u>...

> *This warranty covers all defects that may arise due to faulty workmanship, provided that these defects are not caused by abuse of the product. Abuse is construed to mean the use of the product during the day or under artificial light—such as during the night. Abuse is also assumed when the product is used by children and/or adults and/or teenagers and/or senior citizens and/or ... [trailing off into illegibility]*

"THE MISERABLY MESSY MESSAGE"

You know something even <u>worse</u>? Like waiting for an important phone message? If so, our advice is never, never leave the house! Not for <u>any</u> <u>reason</u>! No, not even if you're up to your chin in flood or fire! <u>Stay there</u>! Or else, one of your parents might take the message for you! And here's what it will probably look like...

SOUNDS TO DIE BY

Not only are there people and things to watch out for, there are also sounds that are out to get you. Here are some examples of those noises that hold you victim.

When some big, tough guy is playing a music box so loud that you can't sleep, you can do one of two things—you can either tell him to "Shut that damn thing off" or try to live with the noise! Let's consider alternative No. 1. If you yell at him, you will achieve quiet—but that quiet will be for eternity, since he will probably <u>kill you</u>. Inasmuch as dead people hear nothing, it's the end of your problem.

But, if you're not ready for that much quiet, better resign yourself to the noise and pray that he'll find another neighborhood to entertain with his free concert...

When you're a teenager you want either of two things. One: to be <u>noticed</u> by everyone, or TWO: to be <u>ignored</u> by everyone. Unfortunately, you can never pick the times nor the places for either! For instance, how many times have you hit a homer when <u>no one</u> was looking? Or fell on your face when <u>everyone</u> was? See?

Now, when you go out to a restaurant with your folks, you want to <u>disappear</u> as fast as you can! Folks are just too embarrassing to be with for any length of time!

But when they insist on taking you out for your birthday, they have ways of guaranteeing that you will be uncomfortable unto death! They instruct the management to have the waiters bring you a birthday cake and then stand around and sing "Happy Birthday" to you in front of dozens of <u>strangers</u>! When this happens you realize that the phrase "Dying of shame" is not a figure of speech, but a valid medical diagnosis!

Plumbing is a wonderful thing! Indeed, it is one of civilization's <u>greatest</u> accomplishments! Let's think for a moment what life would be like if we <u>didn't</u> have plumbing! In fact, <u>you</u> think—it's too disgusting for us to waste our valuable time on!

However, there are few more annoying accomplishments of civilization than plumbing that goes <u>wrong</u>! And when is the worst time for it to go wrong? In the middle of the night! And that brings us to the subject, "Sounds!" Is there a more annoying sound than a toilet in the dark of night that refuses to stop flushing? Maybe there is one—the sound of someone else going to the bathroom late at night and your <u>not</u> hearing the toilet flush ...

There is one sound that can rob a teenager of the <u>will to live</u>! That sound is usually made by a parent who has no idea of the deadly consequences! That sound conveys the words, "Your father wants to talk to you!"

On the face of it, those words shouldn't carry such destructive weight! But think about it! What father ever wanted to talk to his kid about something <u>good</u>, <u>positive</u> or <u>happy</u>? The simple fact is that there are no words in the adult lexicon to express satisfaction, approval, or affection toward one's child! You see, language is merely a tool which people use to express something that already exists.

What more can we say? If Elizabeth doesn't leave before the sun sets, she's definitely a tough cookie. If she stays, she can never be sure that the next guy who asks her for a date wasn't hanging around the pharmacy when the druggist broke the news!

BE KIND TO DUMB ENEMIES DEPT.

Up to now we've been pretty rough on parents, brothers, sisters, and all those other seemingly useless members of society whom we bump into from time to time. But let's give the devils their due! Some of our enemies are really <u>good</u> at what they do—making our lives <u>miserable!</u> And why shouldn't we recognize and <u>award</u> people when they do something well? (If this doesn't make any sense to you, do not become alarmed, it means you're following right along! If it <u>does</u> make sense, you're in <u>trouble!</u> But not so bad that a simple remedy—like buying some extra copies of this book—won't cure! Of course we're still trying, boob!) So without <u>further</u> ado … on second thought, how about a <u>few more</u> "ado's"? Ado, ado, ado, … okay, so with <u>three more</u> ado's, let's get on with this silly business…

Academy Awards For

THE
ALFIE

MIES

We all know Academy Awards are given for the best <u>acting</u> <u>performances</u> of the year! But those people get <u>paid</u> for acting, so they <u>should</u> be good! <u>Big deal</u>! The folks who <u>really act</u> because they <u>love</u> to, are the everyday clods like teachers, parents, dentists, etc. They act as if they're your <u>friends</u>! Are they? Hah! <u>Double</u> hah! But their acts are terrific—they fool you <u>most</u> of the time! So here we go, after, say, <u>two more</u> "ado's"…

The first people we are here to honor are perhaps the **finest** actors we will ever meet in everyday life—our children's **teachers**! In the category, "**Overworked**," the winner is Ms. Emma Carnuba! And here is a scene from her award winning performance! Roll the film, please...

In the **Dentist's Competition**, the first winner of an Academy Award is Dr. Irving Sputum for his memorable performance in "**Who Did That Rotten Dental Work Before You Became My Patient?**"

And the winner for his bewitching performance in "The Big Cover Up," is Daniel Herley.

Do you want your kids to see male and female dogs running around with their wee wees hanging out? We demand that the dirty minded people at Disney Studios recall these kind of films and re-edit them. We further demand that they not only cover up animal sex organs but also flowers which are nothing more than vegetable sex organs!!

BAN NUDDITY